A Thankful Heart
Tanka after Ninety

Cathy Street

A Thankful Heart
© 2015 by Cathy Street
Cover image & illustrations © 2015 Amy Claire Rose Smith
Photographs © 2015 Joy McCall

All rights reserved. No part of this book may be reproduced except for brief passages for the purposes of an article or review.

"God bless us, every one!"

~Tiny Tim

from Charles Dickens' *A Christmas Carol*

Some of these tanka have appeared, or are forthcoming, in *The Bamboo Hut*, *Bright Stars* and *Skylark*.

who's script is this,
green on the inner petals
of every snowdrop?
all the angels I have known
were of this earth

~for Cathy & Joy

Tanka by Claire Everett, first published in *Skylark* 2:1, Summer 2014

Introduction

Tanka, meaning 'short song' is the modern equivalent of *waka*, a traditional Japanese lyric poem that can be traced back some 1300 years. From the compositions of the 8th century Heian Court through the Edo period (19th century), *waka* was largely composed by the aristocracy, although the *Man'yōshū* ('Collection of Myriad Leaves'), included the affairs of ordinary people among its themes, alongside laments for the dead, declarations of love and longing and sketches that sought to capture the ephemeral nature of the natural world. Contributing poets included fishermen and soldiers as well as nobles and emperors. In the late 19th century, Western poetry was introduced to Japan through translation and with it came greater freedom of expression and the potential to write about concerns more relevant to the common man, or woman. Under the influence of reformists like Tekkan, Akiko, Shiki and Takuboku, increasingly modern themes were tackled via this traditional form. For contemporary tanka poets pretty much "anything goes."

When Joy McCall showed me this collection of tanka composed by her mother in her tenth decade, I couldn't help but wonder what some of the early writers of *waka* would make of the fact that not only has this beautiful and malleable form stood the test of time, it has washed up on Western shores and become everyday practice for many for whom poetry, as taught in school, was something of a chore. Cathy tells us she enjoys writing, that "ideas come quickly" and often, despite it being past her bedtime she is eager to commit them to paper. She speaks of her faith, her family, the passing seasons and the creatures that visit her garden.

A Thankful Heart

There is much happiness to be found in simple pleasures like eating fish and chips on the seafront — how much better they taste straight from the paper, rather from a plate at the dinner table! Particularly moving are her observations about her daughter's poetry. She is not only proud of Joy's achievements, she also finds her strength in the face of illness and disability inspiring and humbling. She tells us how Joy's tanka stir the emotions and that she reads each poem twice in order to remember it. One doesn't doubt that they are as much a part of her as the badges of old age, the scars of child-bearing. As we get better acquainted with Cathy through her straightforward tanka, we begin to see how Joy — so prolific in the contemporary English-language tanka community — has inherited her mother's love of the natural world, her kindness, resilience and fortitude. Equally, how validating it must have been for Joy to not only have her mother take such an interest in her creative life, but be so inspired by it she takes up the pen herself!

Joy tells me her mother never kept a diary and remained very active until her nineties. That is when she began writing tanka. She created, in a few short years, a wonderful legacy for her children, grandchildren and the generations to come. Simple as Cathy's tanka are, they highlight how accessible and therapeutic the form is and demonstrate its potential to serve as personal memoir. Many small incidents and observations that would otherwise have been lost have been preserved for posterity. At a time of her life when Cathy might have been expected to be experiencing lapses of memory or diminishing mental acuity, she was composing 5/7/5/7/7 tanka on a regular basis and clearly enjoying it — a refreshing change from the crosswords and sudoku recommended by doctors as excellent ways to keep an aging mind agile.

In an era when mindfulness has become something of a buzzword, this nonagenarian was already well-versed in the concept and was very likely the oldest tanka poet writing in English in the world. I imagine that Cathy would have been oblivious to this and it is that lack of self-consciousness that imbues her tanka with an almost childlike innocence.

From what Joy has told me, wherever her mother is, if she knows her collection of later-than-late-in-life tanka has reached a wider audience, she'll be doing a "happy dance."

~Claire Everett, Founder & Editor of *Skylark*

Cathy Street

My wee bungalow
is part of sheltered housing
for the elderly.
It's like a little village.
We're all good friends together.

Old age is good fun
if you don't feel guilty for
dropping off to sleep
after your morning breakfast,
not waking up till lunch-time.

A Thankful Heart

The cheeky squirrel
hops onto the bird table
and has a good feast
while the birds wait patiently
to see if anything's left.

The thrush has nested
in the hedge at the bottom
of the long garden
soon the young thrushes will hatch
and they will all be hungry.

The parent birds will
be kept busy finding worms
and slugs to feed them,
and will go hungry themselves
to feed their growing fledglings.

Why does the squirrel
bury nuts, and then forget
where he has put them?
During the winter, they will
take root and become nut trees.

Outside, it's windy
and the rain is pouring down,
but in my warm room
I sit by the cosy fire
and praise God for my wee home.

I wake each morning
to the sound of the pigeons
cooing in the oak tree
outside my bedroom window:
it must be time to get up.

The ground is so dry.
We badly need lots of rain.
The clouds blow past us
but we miss the rain again.
I must go fill the birdbath.

A Thankful Heart

Norwich is too far
for me to drive my scooter,
but a free bus pass
makes the trip a real pleasure,
passing through the countryside.

The baby squirrels
have just come down from their drey
in the old oak tree.
They scamper across the lawn.
What a pity one gets old.

I look forward to
the apples in the orchard
being ready to pick.
Some I shall store for winter
and some I shall enjoy now.

When I was younger
I could ride my bike to town,
but now my scooter
soon takes me down to the shops.
Growing old can be good fun.

I can't remember
if I mentioned the bluetits;
they use the nest-box
in the old plum tree each year.
This year seven bluetits hatched.

A Thankful Heart

Tonight the sea's rough.
Will the lifeboat be called out
or will the sailors
get home safely by morning,
with their boats laden with fish?

I've been invited
to a friend's birthday party.
I wonder who else
will be there? It should be fun.
I have her present ready.

Out in the garden
I saw a caterpillar
eating a green leaf.
I looked, there were many more
eating the leaves, one by one.

Today in Dereham
I was glad to meet a friend
who I had not seen
for ages. In the café
we had a cup of coffee.

I do love Cromer.
It has everything you need:
a clean sandy beach,
the pier, and a lovely church,
and Cromer crabs are famous.

It wasn't raining.
I went to a car-boot sale,
bought a teddy bear.
I found another small bear;
I went home with the three bears.

A Thankful Heart

The gardens are dry;
we've had no rain for three months;
the lawn is all brown.
At last, the barometer
is falling to Changeable.

We did our shopping
and I got some real bargains.
It's lovely to have
the larder stocked up again
with all my favourite things.

At the charity shop
I bought a blue cardigan.
It matches my skirt.
I shall wear it tomorrow
because it has turned cooler.

It's really bed-time
but I so enjoy writing;
ideas come quickly
and I want to write them down
or I shall soon forget them.

It's warm and cosy
sitting by the fire tonight.
My chair is comfy.
I'll make a cup of tea and
settle down for the evening.

A Thankful Heart

My friend wrote to me.
I was glad to hear from her:
I was wondering
if she had forgotten me —
she didn't write at Christmas.

The apple blossom
in the orchard was lovely;
better this springtime
than last year, so we should have
a bigger crop of apples.

I went for a drive
through the Norfolk countryside.
Dog-roses were out,
and the cow-parsley as well.
It was a beautiful day.

I enjoy Sundays;
it's a day to worship God
and not feel guilty
to make it a day of rest —
Monday will come soon enough.

A party is planned.
I wonder who will turn up?
Friends and relations
from far and wide will arrive;
so good to see them again.

A Thankful Heart

At last it has rained;
the dry ground has soaked it up.
How welcome it is.
I hope it will rain all night,
the farmers will welcome it.

I went to the sea.
It was a lovely fine day.
We went for a swim
and the water was quite warm,
then we had our picnic lunch.

In my back garden
I saw a blue butterfly,
the first one I've seen.
It didn't stay very long.
I hope it will come again.

Why do fish and chips
taste better by the seaside
wrapped up in paper
rather than a proper plate
set on a dining table?

My new friend gave me
a slice of home-made cheesecake.
She is a good cook
and accomplished in many ways —
a most unselfish person.

A Thankful Heart

A peacock landed
on my summerhouse today;
where did he come from?
Does he know his way back home
where his peahen waits for him

I have been cooking
in my kitchen this morning.
Now it's ten o'clock
and I am tired already:
I must be getting old!

The postman's just been;
time to stop work and read mail:
two letters from friends
and the rest is all junk mail
to go to be recycled.

'Anyone at home?'
The door opens and my friend
pops in to greet me.
I make us mugs of coffee
and we sit and chat.

A Thankful Heart

Dark clouds overhead.
Was it a plane I heard or
rumbling of thunder?
I wish it would rain all night
and tomorrow the sun would shine.

I'm having lunch out.
I can't decide what to choose.
I like roast chicken
but I like fish and chips too.
Maybe I'll choose shepherd's pie.

I wonder why Peter
fell in love with me at all?
I'm so glad he did
because I loved him dearly,
we were happy together.

A mouse is living
under my summer-house floor.
I'll put some cheese out
because I love to see him
pop out and gobble it up.

A Thankful Heart

My back aches tonight.
I've worked hard in the garden.
I'll have an early night,
take it easy tomorrow,
write some overdue letters.

We went for a drive
in the country this afternoon.
Lambs played in the fields.
Dog-roses bloomed in the hedgerows.
It was a lovely warm day.

God's so good to me
and I can depend on Him
to take care of me
now that my darling husband
has died and I live alone.

I'm never lonely.
My wee home is so cosy;
friends often pop in,
my family come to see me
which is always a great joy.

Cathy Street

As I wake refreshed
after a very good sleep,
I look out to see
If the sun's shining. If not,
I go back to bed again.

It's a sunny day,
just right to dry the washing.
It's soon on the line
and blowing in the warm breeze.
I'll iron it tonight.

A Thankful Heart

The duck has laid eggs
under a bush in my garden.
I watch when she leaves
the nest, and take an egg
to scramble for my supper.

My friend is happy,
she's expecting a baby.
Her husband is pleased;
they both want a big family,
so I'm busy knitting things.

I love her tanka,
they stir my emotions.
Sometimes I weep and
sometimes laugh, always thinking
I so admire her courage.

Her words make sense.
They are wise and loving.
I read them twice
as they are worth repeating;
then I remember them.

What she writes now
are deep thoughts, like some
flowing clear river
full of love and peace, going down
to the sea of experience.

A Thankful Heart

My neighbour is ill.
I wish I could help her more.
In spite of her pain
she's remarkably cheerful
and so grateful for any help.

I watched a spider
weave her web beautifully.
It seems such a shame
to spoil such a work of art
so I shall let it stay there.

Every other year
the Bishop of Norwich invites
his retired clergy
to lunch at the Bishop's House.
It's a great get-together.

My door was open
so a young squirrel popped in
and he looked around
then he decided to go
out where he belonged again.

A Thankful Heart

To be a Christian
you swim against the tide
like a silver minnow
in a fast-flowing river
going down to the great sea.

Today is Sunday.
A day to rest and relax
and I shall praise God
for His love and care for me
every day of the past week.

I love Christmas time
because I get news of friends.
Some news is so sad.
I pray for them and write back
a letter of sympathy.

I get some letters
full of joy and gratitude:
a new baby born,
a successful operation
or good news of other kinds.

I watched a large rook.
He dropped a big crust of bread
into my birdbath.
I threw it onto the lawn.
The small birds soon ate it all up.

Next week I'm going
with Joy and Andy to see
the church on the hill
at Shotesham, and after
we shall have lunch at the pub.

A Thankful Heart

My doorbell didn't work
so my friend 'Alf' mended it.
How often my friends
pop in just when I need them.
I hope I'm a good neighbour.

The usual postman
is like a ray of sunshine.
His cheery greeting
would always light up your day.
He's always such a happy man

Cathy Street

I woke this morning
wondering what day it was;
just then the phone rang —
Charles, offering a ride to
the Salvation Army coffee morning.

At the sale, I bought
a home-made bacon and egg flan.
I shall eat one half,
and give the rest to my friend —
it's too much for one person.

I lay in my bed.
It was raining hard outside.
I was cosy and warm.
I felt sad for the homeless;
why have they no home to share?

A Thankful Heart

What a lovely day
Wednesday turned out to be.
I had nothing planned,
but friends dropped in for coffee
and took me for a drive out.

I enjoyed my fish
in parsley sauce for supper,
I had it with peas
and fresh-dug new potatoes —
just what I fancied tonight!

Cathy Street

I miss my Peter
'though he died ten years ago.
Together we had
a good life, a happy marriage
from beginning to end.

I have three grandsons
and seeing them growing up
has been so lovely.
They are all so different
And I love them all dearly.

Our two grand-daughters
grew up in far Canada.
Sometimes we flew there
to visit them, or they came
to see us. Such happy times!

A Thankful Heart

The barometer
has gone back to Changeable —
rain is on the way.
I'm glad, because the farmers
badly need a good night's rain.

I shop on Wednesdays
so today my larder is full,
and my fridge-freezer.
There's not much left in my purse!
I must soon go to the bank.

People are so kind:
they offer to post my letters;
one picked me roses,
they are deep red and smell lovely;
they sit on my windowsill.

Cathy Street

I had a phone call
from an old friend in Carlisle;
I got all the news —
the church is still doing well,
you get such a warm welcome.

Nesta's a good friend.
She's been baking cakes today.
She baked one for me,
a lovely cherry fruitcake —
I shall ask some friends to tea.

A Thankful Heart

We lived at Lowestoft
and loved being by the sea.
We moved to Carlisle
and although we missed the sea,
we liked climbing the mountains.

I treated myself
to a new recliner chair.
After lunch each day
I have an hour's rest in it,
and sometimes even two hours!

    I'm going shopping
    tomorrow, and I've written
    a long list of things.
    I hope I did not forget
    any important items.

        It was a grand day.
        I did so many small jobs
        which needed doing —
        I've been putting them off, so
        I'm satisfied with my day.

            I'm looking forward
            to going to the party
            on this Saturday.
            Nearly all the family
            will be there, and many friends.

A Thankful Heart

We kept a goat
called Polyanna, when we lived
in Cambridge. Goat's milk
makes lovely cheese, and I like
it to drink, and for cooking.

Turning out a drawer,
I came across a jumper.
It was a favourite,
I must have had it for years.
It's red, and I still love it.

I noticed today
that the plums were ripening.
Some are red already
and soon they will turn purple.
This year the tree is loaded.

This year, my neighbour
has a wasps' nest in her roof —
last year, I had them.
I wonder why they left my roof
and went to her roof instead?

A Thankful Heart

It must be a sign
of old age when you drop off
to sleep as soon as
you sit down to read a book . . .
and the book falls on the floor.

Food prices are up
but my pension is the same.
By shopping carefully
I have all I need each week
and can still balance the books.

I do love Sundays,
and the service this morning
was full of praises
to our wonderful God, and
we sang such beautiful hymns.

The nest-box behind
my summerhouse was occupied
this year by coal tits.
Today I saw six fledglings
and they were all so tiny.

The TV news was
all so very negative,
doom and gloom all through,
all except for the weather forecast —
and that was 'warm and sunny'.

A Thankful Heart

I always like it when
I do all I planned to do.
I go to bed satisfied;
then I lie in bed, and plan
what I must do tomorrow.

I have too many
clothes and shoes in my wardrobe;
I don't need so many
so I shall have a turn-out
and go to the charity shop.

Cathy Street

I walked by the sea
and the tide was going out.
the little rock pools
were full of tiny creatures:
crabs, seaweed and silver fish.

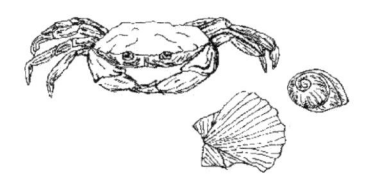

One Saturday night
in February 1953,
the high tide flooded
the beach village at Lowestoft.
Praise God, no lives were lost.

A Thankful Heart

The sunset tonight
was truly spectacular.
The sky was aflame:
red sky at night, shepherd's delight —
it should be fine tomorrow.

My mother-in-law
was such a good friend to me.
I looked after her,
and when she died, I was sad
because I lost a dear friend.

I looked out last night
before I drew the curtains
and to my surprise
I saw a hedgehog walk by
on my lawn, in the moonlight.

Cathy Street

I'm glad my youngest
daughter Ruth lives by the sea.
When I visit her
I have a day by the sea —
and a good meal out, as well.

I'm glad my eldest
daughter Joy lives in Norwich.
We go out to lunch
at a good riverside pub,
and I can see the city.

I'm glad my son David
comes so often to see me.
We sit and drink tea
and catch up on all the news
of his work and his family.

A Thankful Heart

God made a good world —
it's all very beautiful.
We must care for it:
one day He'll come back again.
We must give account to Him.

We are all sinners
but some have been forgiven:
they'll go to Heaven.
Others will not acknowledge
their sin, and will go to Hell.

Cathy Street

I was looking through
some photo albums today,
when I found a snap
of me in school uniform —
did I really look like that?

I found another
photo of our wedding group.
Now, we are all old.
Some keep in touch with me still.
We must be all ninety now.

I used to cycle
to school on my bike each day.
There were no buses
that would have been convenient,
but I did enjoy the ride.

Peter and I went
to Branscombe for our honeymoon.
We stayed at a farm.
The farmer's wife was so kind
and cooked us some lovely meals.

A Thankful Heart

I had a letter
from a most dear friend today.
It was such good news —
she'd come home from hospital
and was feeling very well.

I often look back
to when my children were home;
we went for picnics
and often picked blackberries:
they were truly happy days.

Cathy Street

My three friends and I
drove out into the country.
We stopped at a café
and all had cups of coffee
and home-made buttered cheese scones.

I sat by the fire.
The wind was howling outside.
I was recalling
all I had managed to do.
I went to bed contented.

Jenny came, to bring
a slab of good carrot cake.
She's a kind neighbour
and always willing to help
and pass on some good news.

A Thankful Heart

I'm feeling lazy.
I can hear the clock ticking.
If I don't start work
soon, I shall drop off to sleep,
and that won't get the work done!

A friend says, honey
is nothing special really,
it's just sugars, spat
from out of a bee's stomach.
I don't agree — I love honey!

I gave up driving
when I was just eighty-two.
I do miss the car
but now with a free bus pass
I can still travel about.

There was a double
rainbow in the sky today.
It was brilliant
against the dark thunderclouds:
I took a photo of it.

A Thankful Heart

My husband and I
once visited relatives
who lived in Sweden.
They made us very welcome
and we enjoyed our stay there.

I had three brothers
but only one dear sister.
Mum and Dad loved us.
We were a happy family;
we had a good start in life.

I was always sure
I wanted to be a nurse.
I trained in London
at the St. James Hospital.
It has helped me throughout life.

Cathy Street

I married Peter.
He was a young clergyman.
We had good parishes:
Norwich, Cambridge, Lowestoft,
then Carlisle and Cheadle Hulme.

We had three children
we loved - two girls and one boy.
God blessed us richly.
We holidayed in North Wales —
a friend lent us his cottage.

A Thankful Heart

I love chocolates,
especially the dark sort.
A day never passes
without me enjoying some.
I make sure I don't run out.

Sue went on holiday
and she came home on Friday.
She brought back for me
a box of Belgian chocolates.
It was very kind of her.

Cathy Street

It's been a nice day
weatherwise — sunny and warm.
I spent the morning
tidying up the garden,
and then took my tea outside.

On Friday I went
to a church coffee morning.
They had some nice stalls.
I bought a home-made fruitcake
and a hand-knitted jumper.

I sent for some shoes
from a mail-order catalogue
and when they arrived
they fitted me perfectly
and are so comfortable.

A Thankful Heart

Times are hard just now;
prices are going up, but
pensions are unchanged,
so how to economise
so we can just break even?

My little plum tree
is loaded with plums this year.
I shall have enough
to share with the family
when they come to visit me.

A friend asked me to
have lunch with her tomorrow.
She made lasagne
and she knows I'm fond of it.
She is an excellent cook.

How I praise my God
for He sends the sun and rain
and gives life to all.
Seedtime and harvest won't fail,
because He said it wouldn't.

A friend came today,
she'd made a chocolate cake.
She's so kind to me.
I'll have a slice with my tea
and ask my neighbour to join me.

A Thankful Heart

My gutters are blocked
with leaves, and it's raining hard.
Water is pouring out.
A duck and seven ducklings
are having a shower in it.

I've done my work now
and I have a free evening.
Nothing on TV,
maybe I'll do some mending
and listen to a CD.

I planted a tree,
a red may, in my garden;
and then I moved house.
The new folk didn't want it
and they dug it up again.

A Thankful Heart

My friend's been away —
I look forward to hearing
about where she went
and all the people she met.
I missed her while she was gone.

In early summer,
blackbirds were feeding their young
who're always hungry.
I found the nest in my hedge.
They build there every year.

I love getting cards
from people on holiday.
One came from Eastbourne.
I once went there for a week
and the sun shone every day.

A baby squirrel
hopped on my birdbath to drink.
He was so tiny —
I've never seen one so small.
I wonder where the drey is?

Cathy Street

The plum tree opposite
my kitchen window, bears well.
This year it's laden
with fruit which is just ripening.
One more week and we'll pick some.

I got a flat tyre
on my scooter last Tuesday.
I soon phoned the shop
and they came out straight away
and soon mended the puncture.

A Thankful Heart

I do appreciate
all the simple things in life:
the starry sky with
the full moon at night in Spring;
and a nice hot cup of tea.

Our God made the world
and it is so beautiful —
we must care for it
and not abuse our heritage.
Our God does love us so much.

God has guided me
every step of the way through life,
and now I am old
I can praise Him for his care
and trust the future to Him.

Afterwords

My mother was an amazing woman who lived a long and happy life and never knew the meaning of the word 'can't'. Her favourite saying throughout her life was 'I can do it' — and so she could, anything she set her mind to do, she did it, usually singing as she worked.

She was a loving mother, not just to her own kids, but to adopted and foster kids who lived with us. She was a fine wife and a great friend to so many people. She made everyone feel welcome and she just accepted people as they were.

It's an old-fashioned saying but she was a blessing to everyone who knew her. No matter what happened in her life, she never complained. She had a simple faith in God and a loving heart.

My mother could turn her hand to anything. She would demolish old walls and rebuild them. She would lay paving slabs. She built sheds, many sheds. She spent hours gardening and knew the Latin names of all the plants. She could recite all kinds of poetry. I got my love of poetry from my mother and from her father, my Swedish grandfather.
She was a trained nurse who worked in a London hospital during the war years and faced bombing, while nursing returning soldiers.

My mother never really retired. She was always taking care of someone or something, always busy, always happy. Her life was all about giving, her love, her time, her practical skills. She knitted blankets all her life and gave them away. Even in her eighties she was still fixing roofs and building sheds and baking pies. As the heaviest lifting became too much, she took up art and made and sold very many lovely paintings. When she turned ninety she said she was going to retire and take it easy. Hah. She began to read my tanka in journals, and started to write tanka, many every day, about her day-to-day life, the nature she loved, the creatures around her, the people she loved, and her constant faith.

She liked traditional tanka and always wrote in 31 syllables, loving to sit and count and speak the poems and write them in her notebooks. She was so thrilled when M.Kei and Steve Wilkinson accepted her tanka for their journals, and I feel so grateful for that, for it brought more joy into her life, and at once she began planning her first book of tanka. She was 95.

Here I need to digress and tell the story of how her life ended. We were visiting her in hospital after a minor stroke and after a few days there, she was about ready to go home again. She had eaten her lunch and was beginning on a chocolate pudding with custard, her appetite always good, when she said 'I'm going to heaven today.' We smiled. She was a long way off being anywhere near dying. I offered to stay with her, wondering. She said 'No, go home, this is between me and my God.' So we left, waving in the doorway and saying 'See you tomorrow.' We got home and as we came indoors the phone rang. It was a bemused nurse to say that right after we left, my mother got onto her bed . . . and died. We turned around and went back to the hospital and her body lay there, peacefully on the bed. But the life, the spirit, the joyful presence of my mother was gone. It was just a husk, an empty shell. Somehow, she left this life in her own time, in her own way; and there are many people who will always miss her.

So now, many thanks to Claire at *Skylark* for publishing her book. I get the feeling my mother is sitting somewhere, smiling happily to herself . . .

Rest in peace, Mum.

~ Joy McCall, Norwich

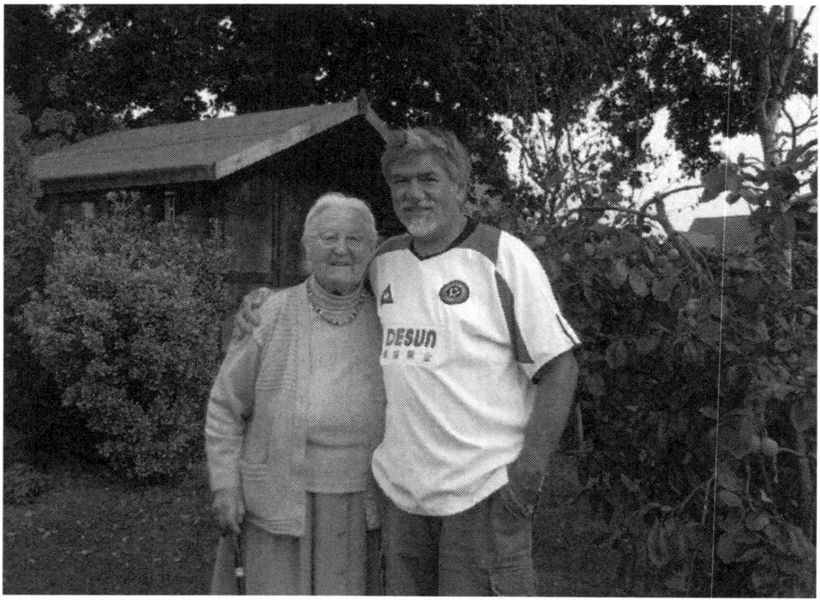
DESUN

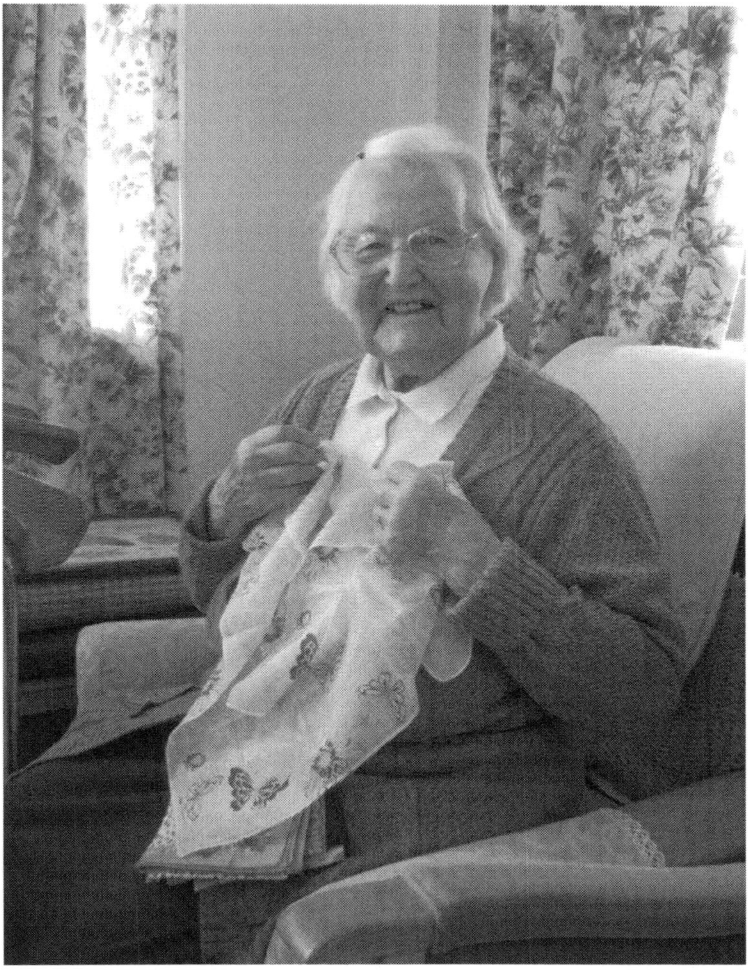

A Thankful Heart

When I met Cathy Street she was ensconced in her favorite chair in a sunny corner of the sitting room at Eckling Grange, the care home where she lived. As she was my good friend Joy McCall's mother, I would occasionally send her cards and small gifts in the mail and she always included me on her Christmas letter list, but it wasn't until March of 2013, when my husband and I made a trip from Canada to the UK, that I finally met Joy's mum in person. I remember she opened with relish the chocolate box we brought with us and shared them round. She hugged me as if I was family. Joy told her that I wrote lullabies for my grandsons and she asked if I would sing one for her mum. I remember the way Cathy leaned in to listen, holding my hand in both of hers, as I sang quietly to her about marigolds and little grandsons dreaming their baby dreams. It was both the first and last time I ever met Cathy Street. What I recall most of that brief meeting was the careful, attentive way she listened, her smiling blue eyes and her gentle ways. She was one of the most genuinely contented people I have ever met. How many elderly people would write "old age is good fun" and truly mean it? She was funny and warm and bright. Cathy Street, like the title of her book, truly did have *A Thankful Heart*. It was a gift to meet her. In this collection of her poems you will be gifted to meet her too.

~Lynda Monahan, author of the poetry collections *A Slow Dance in the Flames*, *What My Body Knows* and *Verge*.

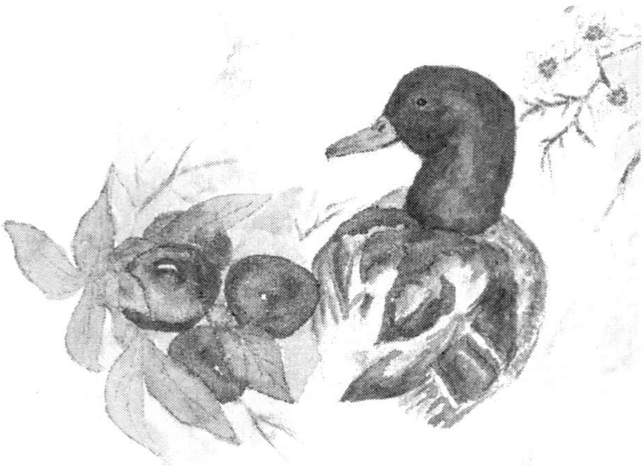

Printed in Poland
by Amazon Fulfillment
Poland Sp. z o.o., Wrocław